Published by
Crown Press LLC
Massachusetts
United States of America

www.martamoranbishop.com

ISBN: 978-0-9840051-2-3

Cover Photo: Marta Moran Bishop

Printed in the United States of America

Cover design by SR Walker Designs

Published by:
Crowe Press LLC
Massachusetts
United States of America

www.crowepress.com
www.martamoranbishop.com

ISBN: 978-0-9840051-2-3

Cover Photo: Marta Moran Bishop

Printed in the United States of America

Cover design by SR Walker Designs
www.srwalkerdesigns.com

A Poet's Journey Emotions

Marta Moran Bishop

This book is dedicated to the to my sister, Helen, who has always been there for me.

Acknowledgements

A special thank you to my husband, Ken and my sisters everywhere, for without their advice and support I wouldn't be as strong as I am today. Nor would this book have been written.

.

An Author's Note

Life carries so many emotions, from the birth of a baby to the death of a loved one. The last few years have been a veritable roller coaster of emotional upheaval.

I have divided this book into six categories.

NATURE: It is here that I find some of my most enjoyable moments. I love to watch birds and cats playing and turkeys wandering around our house, peeking in windows.

After a rainstorm, I adore seeing rainbows cover the sky and puddles on the ground begging to be jumped in.

At times, my imagination will take me away to lands I only dream of such as in "The Yeti Scream in Pure Delight." Nature is a fabulous way for me to express emotions.

LOVE: I write about both the highs and lows of love. When I love, I am at my most vulnerable: sinking to depths of despair or flying to heights of passions.

VILLAIN OR HERO: We all have moments when we don't act our best. Life gives us the option of being a villain or soaring upward and becoming a hero.

DEATH: The last few years I have lost loved ones and others I care for suffered serious illness. Because of the depth of loss, I questioned my own feelings about death. When it is my turn to die, how I will I deal with it. It is difficult to imagine. We all want to believe in a forever.

REBIRTH: With luck, we don't stay in the land of the cynic, nor dwell on death or despair, but move forward into happiness and joy.
I hope to remember what I have learned and take the best parts of those I loved with me into the future.
SILLY ME: In order to survive this emotional year I needed to find silly and humorous things. At times, it was difficult, and I found it necessary to seek these moments.
I believe is it is in how we deal with our emotions that make us who we are.
I have been fortunate. Many people have been there for me. Some did so knowingly, and others are unaware that their kindness aided me.
While my experience has been both rewarding and painful with the social media, it is there that I have found some of the best people I have ever known.
Since there isn't space to thank everyone, I hope you will all know how much you mean to me.

A Poet's Journey

Emotions

Contents

Contents

NATURE

FRIENDS OR FOES?

Playing chase me bird
In the sky there flew
Hawk with wings of gold
And a black bird too

Shadows high above
Cast darkness below
The two appear friends
But maybe they're foes

THE NURSE MARE

All alone is the mare
With none around who care
No real place to call home

Pulled away from her herd
Not even a jaybird
To keep her all right
On this dark moonlit night

THE TREE

Powerfully the sun shines
On the leaves of green and gold
Bring the tree vigor and life
Give it the strength to blossom

A place for the bugs to crawl
And a shelter for the squirrels
Birds nest in its limbs so high
In tree houses children play

How bleak the world with no tree
No green boughs to sit under
None to whisper to the wind
As leaves rustle and birds sing

RAINBOWS

Sometimes it's a smile
Often just a grin
Then there's a giggle
A chuckle or two

For rainbows are gifts
Forever a light
To give us all joy
Splendor and hope

WINTER

In sunlight's glimmer
Icicles shimmer
The bare branches clothed
Are heavily bowed

Newly fallen snow
The piles do grow
Sparkling all white
They reach such a height

The weather so cold
Is getting real old
Gray days and snow fall
Are losing their pall

THE TWO WHO WERE ONE

Upon the hill, beside the road
Stood two little trees side by side

Over the years they grew as one
Their trunks and branches intertwined

One hundred years and more they stood
Limbs locked in a lovers embrace

Look closely if you want to see
How long these two have grown as one

They lost a friend a year ago
He stood upon the hill near them

One hundred years and more they stood
The two who were one and their friend

Age is showing some limbs dying
Still they hold each other entwined

Their leaves still shade us in the spring
In fall they turn red, orange, and gold

It's in the winter you will see
The hundred years and more they stood

THE YETI SCREAMS IN PURE DELIGHT

Winter brings its own kind of life
The Yeti screams in pure delight

The mountains talk, the glaciers walk
The hunters' prowl and the wolves' growl

The hawks fly and the eagles soar
The woods are dark and terror reigns

Over the plains, above the hills
The cold wind howls and snow grows deep

The Yeti screams in pure delight
Wolves' prowl, hawks fly, and eagles soar

THE FORTY-NINE FORD

She was an old girl when we met
Time for the junk heap, not in her prime
Lost and alone behind newer models
She sat by herself buried in dust

Once she'd been the toast of the farm
For sixty odd years she'd been enough
Clearing the fields, turning the soil
She had grown old and couldn't keep up

The others had found her lacking
Making her cynical of us
But we were in love, we understood
Older is just a little slower

LOVE

LOVE'S TRUE FREEDOM

Climbing, soaring, flying high
Over hills I glide upon
Sunlight's rays of golden joy

Falling, finding wings again
Into blue skies through the clouds
Blithe, freedom is loves true form

No tears, no fears in one's core
Through light hope is carried now
No fog or darkness clouds me

MOONLIT NIGHTS

A minute ago I heard you
It was just the wind whispering
I still hear your voice in my ears
Only the breeze moving the leaves

Walking down city streets at night
I see you under the moonlight
Much too far away to touch
Until the final wall comes down

You aren't there, except in my heart
Save for those of us, who believe
Spirit lives on and touches us
In the wind on moonlit nights

MY DEAREST EDGAR

I've read your post of yesterday
More times than I can count or say
I cannot seem to speak or hear
Except your words within my ear
What do you mean by nevermore
My heart, my soul that I adore

Where is my love of latter day
Who spoke of dreams that made me stay
We will be one through thick and thin
Nary a word from kith or kin
Could part our hearts and souls once more
I pray to all that doth remain

That mean you, not in your refrain
Nevermore is not meant for me
But some form of insanity
That your temperance has not detained
Your love for me your Emily

DEAR EDGAR

Papa sent a new suitor by
To tempt me though I don't know why

I think he believes I will find
Someone who'll make me want to bind
My heart, my soul, my very mind

He can't know I would rather die
Then take a husband less than me

Each one I give a flower to
I watch them, will they get the clue
Petals all closed, can they see through

Just who I am and what I want
For love is not something to vaunt

To date all have seen a sliver
Look at the flower and quiver
They see not woman or lover

But a female to play mother
Give up their life for another

Oh Edgar beloved lover
Pray I, you'll choose to discover
It's me, you need not another

Please say you not that I'm too young
That your moods would make me unstrung

We two could share life together
Through good and bad we would weather
I Emily wouldn't tether
My Edgar my love forever

WALLS

I thought my heart had hardened
Long past the time for love

Never again let one in
Funny how wrong I was

Believed all my guards were strong
Yet, you got past my walls

How did you do it my love
Get behind the stockade

FIRE WITHIN

Fire within just embers now
No air to fan the flame to life
The tinder box is empty too

Alone you can't relight the blaze
When life is gone, and love is lost

Without the air embers will die
Love is gone without tender care
Learn the art of letting hurt go

To forever keep the flame bright
So love will last and not be lost

ALWAYS

A lifetime ago
We came together
Parted, met again

My heart doth cling
My soul does fill
My spirit sings
My body stills

I hear your voice
I see your smile
Our eyes will meet
The years are gone

Ripples down my spine
Binding me to you
Today, tomorrow
Always for all days

THOUGHTS OF YOU

Thoughts of you drift through my mind
Running rampant of their own accord
Weaving in and out of consciousness

Possessing life of their own
I cannot stop them, control them
Even during day to day living
They won't cease their incessant chatter

Will reality of you
Increase this insanity of thought
Or bring an unhappy conclusion

VILLAIN OR HERO

ENOUGH

Enough, I say to mind games
Gaslighting is so shameful

I do not have time for you
If you can't say I'm sorry

Instead try to cover up
Your own lack of honesty

If you have something to say
Spit it out or go away

I won't play these games of yours
I am not a simple twit

Do not presume you know me
Or analyze or judge me

If you were truly a friend
There would be no need of this

INVISIBILITY

Like a shadow I move through world
Invisibility around me
My past hopes and dreams have gone away
New ones I must make or I'll decay

Somehow alone I'll hold my head high
Keep my honor till the day I die
Heart and spirit kept clean when attacked
Childlike innocence persists intact

Shadows around me defeat me not
Invisibility is my lot
My world gone, a new one I will build
Dreams I'll make, my soul newly fulfilled

JEALOUSY

I don't understand jealousy or focused cruelty
What time is spent on this, could better be spent usefully
Choose instead to proudly live and become the best you can be
Oh can't you see what evil lies in being a bad penny
These games you play make no sense to me

Nor losing your sense of joy with needless complications
In the end, it is you that is hurt by your jealousy
Instead you could find your happiness in what you can be

BETRAYAL

I thought we were sisters
I thought we were friends
Believing the adage
That sharing brought trust

Only you're never wrong
And always are more
Be it pain or glory
You must be supreme

Can never be a case
Of each being right
Can't just be different
Suffering as strong

I must always be less
Or you can't be grand
I can only triumph
If you couldn't care less

You'll make sure I look bad
Always in the wrong

Instead you must trample
If I do too well

All must love you the most
Or you will destroy
Anyone in your way
Leave hurt in your wake

I know the shame is mine
I opened that door
Giving my trust again
Alas, I was wrong

To the bone I am cut
But never again
We cannot be sisters
Nor can we be friends

Your idea of friends
And mine don't agree
For friends do not destroy
Each other for not

VALIDATION

How are you? Someone will ask.
Passing by to their next task
It's just a platitude
No care just attitude

Where has all the niceness gone
When did life become such a con
Will we someday learn fresh
Validation's the bond

Brings us to a high plane
Giving us all greater gain
Caring and thoughtfulness
Not hopeless pointlessness

Validation it is true
Gives back the best of you
Takes away hurt and pain
Frees the world of its bane

TRAUMA DRAMA

Trauma drama I'm sick of you
I'm weary of all your chaos

I'd just as soon you go away
Don't come back on another day

If someone brings you around me
They can just go home and calm down

We all cry and have sleepless nights
To prolong is not my style

Life holds too much beauty and joy
To spend it all in tears and angst

LOVES TO PLAY THE VICTIM

Where does the person come from
Who looks to play the victim
Do they believe one will come
With more friends that they can win

Dwell they still on memories
Slights and hurts from yesterday
Do they keep a diary
Looking for someone to pay

Does this past remembering
Of a slight small as can be
Help them in dismembering
Find more ways to fight and flee

We must keep from becoming
A chum caught up in their net
Keep ourselves free from numbing
To those who truly should get

All help and strength we can give
To those who are the victim

Who look for ways to forgive
Those who have caused them such pain

For they fight for clarity
A way to forgive and pray
Not sink into memory
Look always to new day

They are not like the other
Dwelling in their past decay
They do not blame their mother
Trying to find a delay

They look deep inside themselves
Try not to fault a brother
Find wholeness and cleansing health
Ask for aid from another

Those we owe our truest help
But to the other nothing

WASTE NO TEARS

Condescending tones
Vague innuendos
Based on guessing games

An acquaintance makes
Mistaken judgments
From knowledge unknown

The advice given
Meant just to frighten
Disguised as friendship

Loss and confusion
Review all you know
Of those you thought friends

Waste no tears on them
Who care not for you
Past a casual nod

Friend or acquaintance
The difference is clear
Fear not the latter
But cherish the friend

THE MAN WHO WAS A DOG

A dog I once knew named champ
About the world he did tramp
Never for long would he stay
But to the moon he would bay

He marked each and every post
With each conquest he would boast
With girls he would play the man
Names by the door in a can

At sixty he's still a dog
Most women thought him a hog
On a bar stool he still sat
He believes he's still the cat

My name is not in his jar
A pretty face in a bar
I saw no matter his name
He didn't rate any fame

There once was a dog named champ
But he was truly a tramp
Hold on to your life girlfriend
For all dogs are not your friends

DEATH

DEATH I AM NOT AFRAID

We met when I was three
Again at twenty-five
Death I am not afraid

When my time comes I'll face
Again your warm embrace
Another world I'll find
Behind that final door

For when you come for me
With this life I'll be done
Just like a worn out dress
That has seen better days

Until that time I'll live
With vim and vigor too
See beauty all around
Live and love unfettered

Of death I am not afraid

A TRIBUTE TO MY MOTHER

You could have rivaled Betty Grable
With the beauty of your legs
Elizabeth Taylor with your eyes
And still come out the winner

I knew a beautiful lady

You gave birth to and raised nine children
Worked three jobs, struggled and scrapped
Then you would dance till dawn, laugh and sing
And home to make us breakfast

I knew a beautiful lady

Daily I watched you growing older
Still fighting to walk and live
Your body wasting before my eyes
We shared the good and bad days

I knew a beautiful lady

I wish you could have seen through my eyes
How attractive you still were
Strong, vulnerable, and stunning too
With a soul overflowing

I knew a beautiful lady

I know you once again dance and run
Walk happily through the hills
See rainbows and bask in sunlight
Flying high on wings of song

I knew a beautiful lady

THE DEAD ARE WALKING

Today the dead are walking
Whispering remember me
They say as they are talking

In the trees they're a stalking
Remember me they all plea
Today the dead are walking

I feel them all a flocking
Calling those who are not free
They say as they are talking

All in the corner gawking
Ask them why and they will flee
Today the dead are walking

See them in the wind rocking
Remember us, who are free
They say as they are talking

Upon the door a knocking
Someday they say you will see
Today the dead are walking
They say as they are talking

I'M NOT READY TO LOSE MY SISTER

I'm not ready to lose my sister
Not one kind, nor gentle part of her
The years of memories wash through me

The world will lose such intelligence
Laughter, gaiety and kindness too
When her light is gone and flame burned out

Alas, for the day her smile dies
When her boundless joy has left this world
And her bright, beautiful heart is gone

I'll keep her splendor forever with me
Allowing exuberance a place
To plant its fertile seed of loving

For when her time here has come and gone
And her kind and gentle soul has left
Loving voice and support has vanished

What she taught will live on forever
And her love of life will carry us
Become a beacon to light our way

I LIVE IN MY HEAD

I can't walk or run, nor dance any more
Nor feel your touch or the wind in my hair
But I can see the beauty of your smile
Still remember the sweetness of your lips

Soar with the eagle, swim with the dolphin
Hear the birds sing and imagine their thoughts
I can run with a horse across the field

My body all broken and shattered now
Yet I live, I think, I imagine life
Our eyes still speak the language of our love

Try not to remember the world that was
Nor the accident that brought me here
I tell you these things with my eyes and heart
No longer can I speak or hear your voice

I miss only the touch and feel of you
Now I run with the horse, fly with the hawk
Swim with the dolphin and glide with the wind

Travel to places I only dreamed of
I live in cultures most people don't see
I live in my head and see with my mind

It's only you and your sweetness I miss

Still I see and smell the grass and flowers
When they wheel me out to the garden room
I still believe that life is beautiful

I think I'll leave this broken body soon
Leave behind this world of pain that is mine
Move through that final door when it opens

I will stop in to see you now and then
I will not forget your sweetness and love
Nonetheless, I will not shirk from the new

For this life is now only in my head
I will miss you, but it's time to move on

I DO NOT WANT TO DIE

I do not want to die
My life barely begun
Hardship has been my lot
Trauma and worry too

My bliss still to be found
The joy each day to see
Burdens all left behind
Not carried all alone

Fly with the hawk above
Ride my horse through the woods
Run with wind in my hair
Soar on heights yet to come

TRANSFORMATION

I run down the street with wings on my feet
I dance every night till three
My hunter and I take hedges and walls
Oh what a joy to be free

Tennis balls fly from racket to racket
Our sailboats hull over keels
The salt spray and air blow wild through my hair
Oh but it's grand to be me

I wake with a start, there's pain in my heart
My pillow covered with tears
Running and dancing are all in my dreams
My hunter just memories

For tennis balls fly and sailboats still sail
And salt spray blows off the sea
Trapped in this body that doesn't perform
Spirit that used to be free

TRAVELED

We traveled a road together
We three each of us alone
Yet all of us together

Sometimes in joy, sometimes in pain
Soar to new heights of passions
Sink to new depths of despair

Discovered new meanings of love
We found new friends in the old
Compassion and hope we had

And some of us learned to care

FREEDOM

I'm not sure what I did
That made friendship grow old
It appears your wish now
Makes separation unfold

We're no longer good friends
Your motivation clear
Without causing trouble
I'll leave you alone now

I will miss you dear friend
'Cause I care very much
Respectfully I go
Leaving freedom behind

REBIRTH

LESSONS OF LIFE

Until today at least
I took the lessons each day
And lived my life without qualms

At least that's what I thought
How blind I was yesterday
Forever thinking I knew all

Now that it is too late
I wish I'd taken the time
And spent each moment I could

Talking, walking with you
Enjoying time together
Basking in our special world

And live each day in turn
I hope this will help me learn
To take the joy that's offered

LIFE'S MIRACLES

Have we lost our ability
To find the wonder in the day
To look upon the sky so fair

Make pictures from the clouds above
See the gentle breeze blow the leaves
Hear the calm voices of the trees

Can we still sit so quietly
As the birds fly and the bugs crawl
Capture fireflies in a jar

Have they become a nuisance now
Not a miracle to the eye
All the simple things nature brings

Is there time to gaze at the stars
Or see the moonlight shine so bright
Witness glory and ecstasy

Anger and tension fills our lives
Killing us with fear and stress
With all the running to and fro

Are we losing our precious time
Using it on television
Always doing always going

No time left to teach our children
Trouble-free fun and banter too
Conversation and simple play

Is it worth the fury and strain
We give ourselves and young ones too
Losing the beauty and splendor

HAND IN HAND

Hand and hand they walked the tor
Clouds above the wind did soar
Laughing over tales of yore
Friends forever walked the shore

Amazing journey they had
More life ahead they're glad
Laughter over lack of rad
What matters the latest fad

WILL WE BE SISTERS?

Will we be sisters
Will we be friends
Can we break the chains
Of stereotype

Let jealousy go
Help each other
Delight in triumph
Bury the hatchet

Honoring us all
With caring ways
Forgo backstabbing
Replace it with joy

Find one another
Sustain and guard
Walking hand in hand
Through life's challenges

ENDLESS

Gently the rose falls from the hand
Goddess of sunlight burns brightly
Time moves through eternity
Endlessly recycling

The gold light darkens with the night
Repeating itself forever
Never the same each day new
Dawn to dusk, then dawn again

With renewal there is change
Ever so slight is the movement
No petal or fold the same
Ceaseless this circle of life

IS IT YOU

Is it because I've matured
A magic age for women
Is it you, the way you are
That sets my senses soaring

Your voice caresses my skin
Your eyes speak of promises
Your voice music to my ears
Of things I've seen in my dreams

SILLY ME

PUDDLES

I saw a puddle it was fine
A splash or two will make it mine

I'll leap, I'll jump, I'll make it spray
Splatter and spurt will make fine play

It matters not I'm sopping wet
Though I don't know why they're upset

For water dries so very quick
And doesn't make me a bit sick

CRAIGWORTH DIMPLETON

Craigworth Dimpleton was his name
Our little gray squirrel had his fame
When out with the girls he would go
Downtown where the beer nuts flow

On a leash so he would not run
Cute and friendly he was such fun
Men would flock, drinks and beer nuts flow
Laughter filled the air with a glow

Bedtime he curled up close to us
Against our bellies without fuss
Before he'd sleep, he had his rite
Then cuddled and slept all the night

Craigworth Dimpleton was his name
The gray squirrel who no one could blame
For holes in the back of the couch
Where he made his own little pouch

Upon our shoulder he would ride
Across the yard and all worldwide
Off to the park it was for him
Letting him jump from limb to limb

Till the day came mom did decide
Freedom was his to live outside

Into the park we let him go
To make friends and run to and fro

Craigworth Dimpleton did remain
A gray squirrel that was very tame
Upon a shoulder he would fly
Causing fuss to the passersby

He lived a long life in the park
All would laugh and make a remark
Of the gray squirrel who was so tame
Craigworth Dimpleton was his name

THE HITCHHIKER

I didn't even know
My little hitchhiker
I never caught his name
Over highways we flew

I was all warm inside
He took his ride outside
Holding on for dear life
To the trunk of the car

Not until I was parked
Did I see the poor thing
Crouched against the trunk rim
All aquiver was he

The tiny little mouse
On unfamiliar ground
Across the car he ran
Upon the grass he jumped

No stop to say goodbye
The petrified mouse flew
Running to get away
As fast as he could go.

Sure wishing he stayed put

And not traveled afar
The little hitchhiker
So far away from home

RED RIDER

Once was a redheaded boy named Ken
For a horse he did have a great yen
Mother and father he begged again
To ride the wind and fight the bad men

Now Ken he wanted to play at war
Just like they did in the days of yore
Their dog was too small, without valor
So he thought till his mind was sore

He came up with the perfect recourse
And used his dog's house to make his horse
Blanket became his saddle of course
Then Ken could play lawman and enforce

He rode like the wind fighting bad men
Through rain and snow again and again
Blanket for saddle he joined huntsmen
Riding his own horse across the glen

A GIRL NAMED RED

Once there was a girl named Red
Who pondered each word that was said
Afraid she would make a mistake
She held close the thoughts in her head
Never an idea did she share

Each day it got much harder
To speak a word from her larder
So now she just sits and listens
All who know her fully agree
Her dialogue is all it should be

She is sought by all
Who say conversation with Red
Is stunning and clever to boot
Lucky are those she chats with
For an evening with Red is a hoot

A BIT OF A BOOKWORM

A bit of a bookworm
A bit of a dreamer
The last picked for the team

Popular I was not
Always too shy for that
Often the odd one out

Friends there were not many
We moved too much for that
Gone before they knew me

I never learned the art
Of being the first to speak
Social times were awkward

My heart is in my throat
On that first encounter
What do I say to them

Those that could be my friend
How do I let them know
Friends mean a lot to me

A bit of a dreamer
A bit of a bookworm
The last picked for the team

LIFE'S CRITTERS

Dad and I went up the street
To get the Sunday papers
We met a squirrel spry and neat
And full of funny capers

Had a nut to throw to him
So carefully I threw it
He scampered up on a limb
And sat right down to chew it

WALK ON THE RAINBOW

We will walk on the rainbow
Brighten our hearts with color
Let it weave in and through us

Watch the moonlight together
As it dances with the clouds
Hands out to one another

SILLIE MILLIE

Sillie Millie couldn't stop
Atop the clothes she would plop

The dryer made a warm nest
She did make an awful mess

Our greatest blessing in life is the ability to care and feel. It is something that should never be taken for granted.

Yes, there is always someone worse off than we may be, but our sense of well-being and self must be allowed to flourish. All of us have a valid place in this world, and none of us can be replaced. We are all unique beings.

The Journey Continues.

Marta Moran Bishop

BOOKS BY MARTA MORAN BISHOP

Innocence and Wonder, like Wee Three: A Mother's Love in Verse, is written from the perspective of a child, and is full of verses that range from bugs, dogs, pigs, and nature. It is a terrific book written to charm and enthrall the child in all of us.

Ms. Bishop, has once again produced a book to entertain those of all ages and help us see the world as a place of wonder and joyful simplicity.

If you enjoyed Shel Silverstein, you will surely fall in love with Innocence and Wonder.

Wee Three: A Mother's Love in Verse, is a collection of poetry and verse written through the perspective of a child. It was begun in 1924 by Ms. Bishop's grandmother, Helen Springer Moran, and finished by Marta Moran Bishop. It is reminiscent of the days before the computer and television, when imagination was the key to a child's mind.

Wee Three, is guaranteed to make you smile, laugh, and remember the days of your own youth.

It is a highly entertaining read for both children and adults and will delight the reader with its simple verses. If you enjoyed, A.A. Milne or Robert Louis Stevenson's children's verses, you are sure to love Ms. Bishop's, Wee Three: A Mother's Love in Verse.

Dinky: The Nurse Mare's Foal, is the story of one little foals fight for survival after being taken from his mother within hours of his birth. Dinky takes us on a poignant trip through the heart and mind of an animal, who was born for the sole purpose of bringing his mother to milk. Considered by the elite of the horse world, to be a by-product, a 'junk foal.'

Dinky's story will resonate with animal lovers, as well as anyone who has adopted. Although a horse, his story has been called an adoption story. The reader can follow him through the heartbreak, cruelty, loneliness, and finally to happiness in his forever home. His story is based on true events, as each event from the moment the author met Dinky actually happened, though it is the author's interpretation of what he might have been thinking and feeling during the occasions described in his story. His early life which is unknown has been fictionalized by the author and constructed through research and imagination.

There are many wonderful animal rescue leagues, who have empathy toward these small animals, however they are not all sympathic to them. Since, Ms. Bishop has no knowledge of Dinky's early

days she used the latter to enhance the strength of his story.
It will break your heart, open your eyes, lift your heart, and teach you much about horses. It is suitable for all ages.

The Between Times:

Marta Moran Bishop takes the reader through a possible future. Unlike Orwell's, Animal Farm and 1984, or Ray Bradbury's Fahrenheit 451, The Between Times is not based on the government 'Big Brother,' but rather it is written using the recent ruling by the Supreme Court that corporations are people. In The Between Times, we are shown the possibility of a world where the poor are considered to be a beasts of burden, good only for the labor they can produce or the war they can fight, to enable the war profiteers to make more money.

Poor women are only useful for breeding and considered to be property of men. There is no real way for the poor, who are uneducated to move up in this society, and the middle class is gone.

In this short novel, The United States has taken a social, economic, and cultural step backwards, to a time when our world consisted of lords and serfs. The only thing that keeps those who are not in the ruling class of the elite going, is the belief in a prophecy, that one day a girl will be born who will have the ability to unite all kindred spirits past, present, and future, to bring change to the world.

A truly amazingly imaginative book.

A Poet's Journey: Emotions, is Ms. Bishop's first book of adult poetry. In its pages, you will find the good, bad, and beautiful of being human. It is divided into six categories, Love, Death, Betrayal, Nature, Villain or Hero, and Silly Me.

The verses include a glimpse into the heart and soul of one woman, who lived through an emotional roller-coaster year, yet retained her ability to see the silly side to things and beauty in the world around her.

If you like poetry, this is the book for you, if you have grown up thinking poetry is difficult to understand, pick this book up for within it, you might find something that will resonate with you.

A Poet's Journey: Sunlight and Shadows:

Marta Moran Bishop continues her journey in Sunlight and Shadows. This book of poetry, unlike A Poet's Journey: Emotions, is a more thought provoking book. In its pages, Ms. Bishop, deals with everything from God, to life after death, war, and the shooting in Newtown, Connecticut. Still she is able to bring to life the beauty and grandeur of her surroundings and make us laugh, cry, think, and feel.

Sunlight and Shadows will once again take you on an emotional journey through life.

The Void:

The Void, the first true paranormal short story written by Marta Moran Bishop. It will take you deep into the mind and heart of someone either living through a serious mental illness or possibly something mysterious and dangerous resides in the void.
Altori's sister disappeared in the void and Altori barely survived it. Will Altori return to the void again, to search for her sister? If she does will she survive?

The Void is reminiscent of Alfred Hitchcock or the Twilight Zone of later days.

www.ingramcontent.com/pod-product-compliance
Lightning Source LLC
LaVergne TN
LVHW030913080826
845145LV00010B/2873

* 9 7 8 0 9 8 4 0 0 5 1 2 3 *